Bedtime Math®

Bedtime Math®

Laura Overdeck

Illustrated by Jim Paillot

Feiwel and Friends

New York

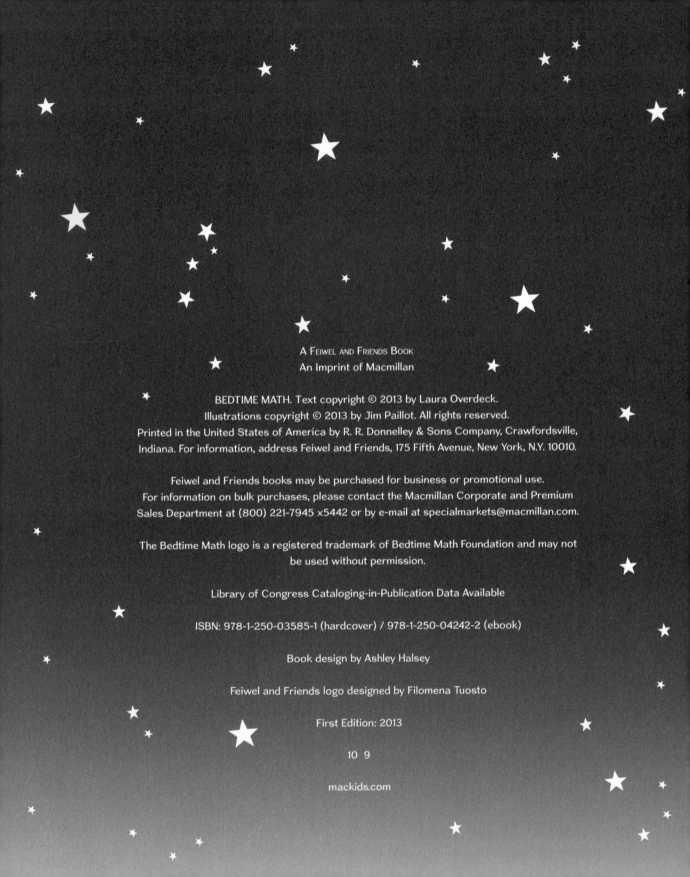

A Feiwel and Friends Book
An Imprint of Macmillan

BEDTIME MATH. Text copyright © 2013 by Laura Overdeck.
Illustrations copyright © 2013 by Jim Paillot. All rights reserved.
Printed in the United States of America by R. R. Donnelley & Sons Company, Crawfordsville,
Indiana. For information, address Feiwel and Friends, 175 Fifth Avenue, New York, N.Y. 10010.

Feiwel and Friends books may be purchased for business or promotional use.
For information on bulk purchases, please contact the Macmillan Corporate and Premium
Sales Department at (800) 221-7945 x5442 or by e-mail at specialmarkets@macmillan.com.

The Bedtime Math logo is a registered trademark of Bedtime Math Foundation and may not
be used without permission.

Library of Congress Cataloging-in-Publication Data Available

ISBN: 978-1-250-03585-1 (hardcover) / 978-1-250-04242-2 (ebook)

Book design by Ashley Halsey

Feiwel and Friends logo designed by Filomena Tuosto

First Edition: 2013

10 9

mackids.com

To Katie, Andrew, and William,
my mischievous math muses . . .
I can always count on you for inspiration.

Introduction

What is Bedtime Math? We all know parents should read to their kids at bedtime, but what about math? Just as reading at home teaches kids to love books, introducing math at home should teach kids to love math, too. Bedtime Math's goal is simple: to make math a fun part of kids' everyday lives, not just something found only in homework assignments. Math should be as beloved as the bedtime story.

So how did Bedtime Math get started? My husband and I, being fans of numbers, started out counting stuffed animals with our oldest child when she was two years old. She totally got into these nightly riddles, so we continued them with our second child. When our third child turned two and started hollering that he wanted a math problem, we realized we were onto something: We had created a flash card-free household where math had become a favorite activity at bedtime. With the encouragement of friends, we decided to spread the word.

It became one of those things that takes on a life of its own. It started one night in February 2012, when I sent an e-mail to ten friends in town with a math problem about short, fluffy, pillow-shaped dogs, inspired by the Westminster dog show. The next night featured NBA players. The third night explored chocolate mousse. Two things happened that week: First, by Friday, the number of friends had doubled, because people heard about the e-mails and asked to join the list. Second, parents said their kids were starting to bug them for a nightly math problem. The kids were hooked. Two weeks later, I set up a Web site, an e-mail marketing program, and a Facebook page, and six months later, we had 20,000 followers, including teachers and principals who were each forwarding the daily math problem to eighty or more students.

The book and the levels. That brings us to this book. I hope *Bedtime Math* gets kids to love math, and maybe gets some of you parents to feel the same way. Each chapter kicks off with a mischief-making topic: extreme vehicles, exploding food—all the stuff we never see in school workbooks. Within the chapters are math stories that lead to three levels of challenge: **Wee ones**, **Little kids**, and **Big kids**, because everyone who opens this book has a different math ability. Readers can tackle as many levels as they like.

Have no fear. The answers appear conveniently on every page, so they're easy to find and you don't have to race to solve them before your child does. Even better, the back of the book lists the math equation underlying each and every math problem, so you can track the math behind the thinking. The goal is to make this easy and fun.

One more thing: It's so important for kids to see grown-ups enjoying math. We never hear educated adults announce, "You know, I'm just not that good at reading." And yet, it's considered perfectly reasonable for those same educated adults to say, "I'm just not good at math." Why? Let's all agree we're never going to say that again— and not in front of the kids! Several parents on the Web site, mostly moms, have said that thanks to Bedtime Math, it's the first time that they're enjoying math. Math is fascinating and cool, and anyone can do it, so let's make sure that's the message we send to our kids.

So . . . how does Bedtime Math work?

How to Do Bedtime Math—The Fun Way

Don't sweat it. Choose the level of challenge that works best. There's a reason we don't list a "correct" age range for each problem. The three levels of challenge are labeled "Wee ones," "Little kids," and "Big kids" precisely to avoid specific ages or grade levels. The first level is named "Wee ones" to emphasize that kids should start doing math as preschoolers. The more math at home before kindergarten, the better. "Little kids" moves your child past counting on fingers to bigger single- and double-digit adding, along with some simple subtraction, multiplication, and logic puzzling.

"Big kids" introduces the excitement of wrestling with bigger numbers—and discovering that they can build on all their little-number learning. All levels, however, are great mental warm-ups for *anyone*, all the way up to the grandparents who use the Web site as a daily brainteaser. So just jump right in, and see what level seems like a comfortable starting point!

It's an activity, not a test. The goal is to have an entertaining conversation that leads to the answer, not to see if your kids can get the answer right off the bat. Read the math problem aloud, then walk through the steps to solve it, and please feel free to give hints when needed.

Don't worry about your kids getting wound up. We haven't seen that happen with Bedtime Math. After all, the time-honored way to fall asleep is to count sheep! Numbers are soothing and predictable, and math problems give kids a reason to settle down and focus.

Besides, what better way to end the day than by accomplishing something?

Don't sweat it, Part II. Yes, we'd love to become part of your routine every single day. But we all have those days that begin with the roof falling through to the first floor, and we just can't quite get to every wholesome activity. *Bedtime Math*—this book, as well as all the content on the Web site—is here for you when you're ready for it.

Any time of day can work. We do talk about nighttime a lot, but Bedtime Math can become a part of any routine: breakfast, carpool, dinnertime, bath time. If you weave it into a daily activity, it can become a natural habit.

Stretch. Because it's a team effort, you can reach as high as you and your child want to try. There's something magical about adding two big numbers for the first time ever, or multiplying 5 times 5. While teachers can't have that playful one-on-one with twenty-three students at once, you *can* do this at home, and you'll find that kids love to tackle the tougher challenge levels.

It's beautiful. Again, we never hear people say "Ewww, a book at bedtime?!" Likewise, there's absolutely no reason to say that about math. Numbers are beautiful, and kids love attention. *Bedtime Math* just puts the two together. With that, let the games begin.

5 10 56 9 6 15 36 125 85 3 8 25

Chapter 1

EXPLODING FOOD

3 1 30 45 103 12 4 72 0 99 21 56

Hot, Hot, Hot

If you've ever bitten into one of those little green bits in a bowl of salsa, you know how hot they can taste. Whoa! They are jalapeños, but they don't even come close to being the hottest peppers out there. The Scoville scale for hotness runs from zero into the *millions*, and on that scale jalapeños rank only a 3,500. Habañero peppers score 350,000, and some peppers actually crack 1 million. If you like feeling as if *you* might explode, there's no end to the level of hot you can taste test.

Wee ones: If you've eaten 3 bites of jalapeño, and you know you can eat 8 bites of them before you just can't take the heat anymore, how many more bites can you stand to eat?

Little kids: If the black pepper you sprinkle on food along with salt ranks just 2,500 for hotness, and the jalapeño scores a 3,500, how many points hotter is the jalapeño?

Big kids: If the jalapeño scores a 3,500 and Tabasco sauce scores a 35,000, how many times hotter than the jalapeño is Tabasco sauce?

Playing Ketchup

We've all struggled to get ketchup out of a glass bottle. That may be why the plastic ketchup squirt bottle was invented. Give it a big squeeze, and you can squirt out a lot of ketchup really fast. When you do, you're packing a lot of tomatoes in that squirt, as every cup of ketchup contains about 14 cooked-down tomatoes. Squirting ketchup is also more fun than throwing a tomato: While a tomato smacking into something might explode and make a mess, ketchup already *is* a mess.

Wee ones: If you squirt 3 squirts of ketchup on a hot dog, and then 1 more squirt on your friend's head, how many squirts did you fire off?

Little kids: If you line up some burgers and squirt ketchup on the 1st burger, then every 3rd burger after that, which burger in the lineup is the 4th burger to get squirted?

Big kids: If you squirt 2 cups of ketchup, and each cup used 14 tomatoes, how many tomatoes' worth of ketchup did you just squirt?

Pop Culture

Whether you make popcorn by heating kernels in an old-fashioned pan or by sticking a bag of them in the microwave, you get the same result: The kernels burst into white fluffs up to 16 times bigger, and become something you can chew without breaking your teeth. The stuff really goes bonkers at the movie theater, where popcorn pops in giant glass boxes, piles up, and then turns toxic orange-yellow when the guy behind the counter adds the "butter." But regardless of the color, when it comes to successful popcorn explosions, bigger is better.

Wee ones: If you stick your hand in the popcorn bag and pull out 10 kernels, but 3 of those kernels never popped, how many good fluffs of popcorn do you get?

Little kids: If you like eating popcorn by throwing it in the air and catching it in your mouth like a seal, and you toss 15 pieces but catch only 9 of them in your mouth, how many pieces end up in your hair and on the floor?

Big kids: If you pop 2 cups of raw kernels in a big movie-theater machine, and all the kernels pop to 13 times their original size, how many cups of popped popcorn come out?

Eggstreme Mess

Pound cake batter needs one egg for every 2 cups of flour. Pancakes use 2 eggs for every 2 cups of flour. Waffles use 4 eggs. You see what's happening here: The more eggs you use, the fluffier the food. Together with yeast, baking soda, and various other ingredients, eggs make food grow in size as it heats up. So you can imagine that if we keep adding more and more eggs, the results could get pretty alarming.

Wee ones: If you need 2 eggs to make 1 batch of pancakes and another 2 eggs for a second batch, how many eggs do you need in total?

Little kids: If tripling the eggs will triple the thickness of your waffles, and a 1-egg batch of batter makes a 10-inch-tall waffle stack, how tall a stack will you get if you use 3 eggs?

Big kids: If you stick a fresh egg in the microwave and heat it for 30 seconds on High, the egg will eventually explode. If you've been microwaving it for 17 seconds already, how many more seconds do you need to make the egg blow up?

Totally Squashed

A large cucumber or a bag of potatoes can get really heavy. That's because veggies are made mostly of water, and water itself is pretty heavy. The veggies at your store, though, are just the normal-sized ones. In places like Alaska and northern Canada, where the summer sun shines for 16 to 20 hours every day, fresh vegetables grow to be *enormous*. Carrots can grow to 2 feet long and squashes can weigh hundreds of pounds—the largest pumpkin ever grown tipped the scales at over 1,000 pounds! Taking one of those home from the grocery store has to be a challenge—whatever you do, don't drop it on your foot.

Wee ones: If you have 4 giant squash and 5 giant pumpkins, how many enormous vegetables do you have?

Little kids: If each giant pumpkin weighs 1,000 pounds and your car weighs 4,500 pounds, how many *whole* pumpkins do you need to outweigh your car?

Big kids: What weighs more, 4 of your 900-pound pumpkins or 5 of your 700-pound zucchinis?

Shaken Bottle

If you ever open a warm soda, watch out, because it could bubble up and fizz all over you. That's because warm soda can't hold air bubbles in the liquid as well as cold soda. You can cause even bigger fizzation if you shake the soda really hard before opening it. The question is, can we do anything useful with that fizz? What if we could power our cars with shaken soda? Cars need a lot of fuel, though . . . if you thought fighting over a soda with your brother or sister could get ugly, try duking it out with your SUV.

Wee ones: If you have 10 cans of soda, but you've kept only 5 of them cold and left the rest sitting in the sun, how many sodas will explode when you open them?

Little kids: If the fizz from 10 sodas can power your car for 1 mile, how far can it drive on 40 sodas?

Big kids: If you have 60 sodas in the car, and you need 42 sodas to fuel your trip to the party and have to share the rest with your buddy, how many sodas do both you and your friend get?

See What Sticks

When you boil a big pot of pasta, and the water starts churning and frothing and making the lid pop off the pot, you have several clues to whether your pasta has fully cooked. Like most people do, you can set a timer and hope your elbows or spirals will finish in the right amount of time. But if you happen to be cooking long, skinny noodles, the surefire way to test their doneness is to throw a few strands against the wall: If they stick, they're soft and bendy enough to eat. Just watch your aim when you throw.

Wee ones: If you throw 9 strands of angel hair pasta at the wall, but only 2 stick to it, how many end up on the floor?

Little kids: If you pull 18 spaghetti noodles from the pot and throw 10 of them to the dog, how many do you have left to chuck at the wall?

Big kids: If your box of linguini supposedly takes 8 minutes to cook, but nothing sticks to the wall and you have to cook it ¼ of that time longer, how many minutes in total will your pasta require?

The 10-Second Rule

So after food explodes all over the floor, you have a very short amount of time to snatch it up and eat it before every possible germ sticks to it. Some people say you have 12 seconds; some say 5; some say it's just 2. No one has *proven* what that amount of time is, though, so everyone has a different opinion. It probably has less to do with how long the cracker or chunk of cheese sits on the floor, and more to do with whether the food is wet and sticks to all the dust and lint down there. But we can all agree that, whether wet or dry, 2 seconds or 10 seconds, food tastes better before it falls on the floor at all.

O Wee ones: If you drop 8 corn puffs on the floor, and your dog snarfs up 6 of them, how many are left for you?

O O Little kids: If you drop crackers on the floor, and you think they become illegal after 12 seconds, and 8 seconds have passed, how many seconds do you have left to rescue those crackers?

O O O Big kids: If you spill 120 Cheerios on the floor—about one bowlful—but half are wet, how many will eventually shrivel up and stick to the floor if you leave them there?

2 83 7 34 22 6 42 116 35 I 14 92

Chapter 2
WILD PETS

5　26　78　51　106　9　27　0　82　37　45

Local Color

Let's face it: Chameleons won't ever win a beauty contest. Their fast-flicking tongues, funny-shaped horns, and eyeballs that roll in separate directions don't make this type of lizard all that handsome. But chameleons can dress up or down better than any other animal. When they sense danger, within a second they can blend into the background by changing their skin color to pink, turquoise, orange, or a host of other funky colors. If you tried changing *your* clothes as fast as your pet chameleon, you'd find the lizard would always win.

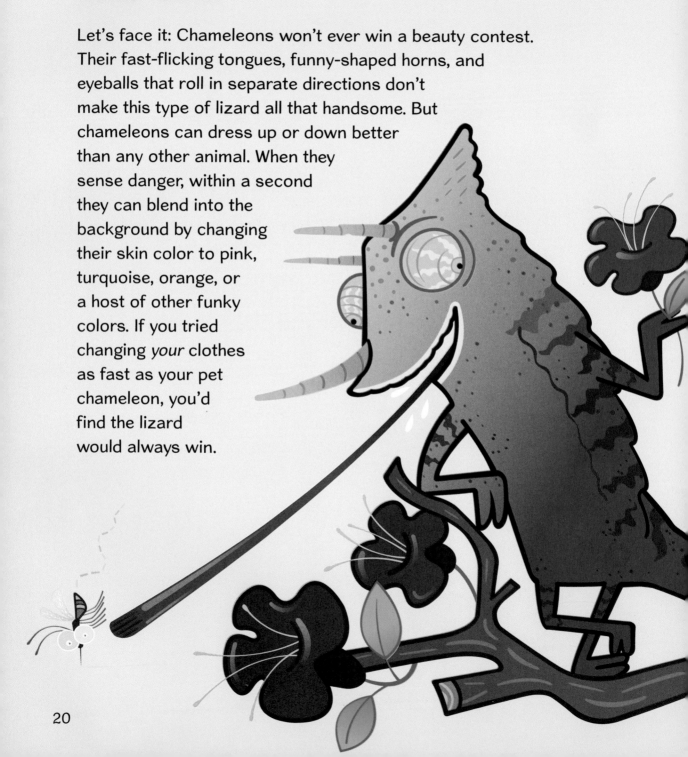

Wee ones: If your pet chameleon has 2 spinny eyeballs, 2 horns, and a really long tongue, how many unusual body parts is that?

Little kids: Chameleons can stick their tongues out *twice* their body length. If your chameleon is 20 inches long, how long can it stick out its tongue?

Big kids: If your chameleon can show off 9 different colors, how many more colors does it need to show off to keep up with your 24-color box of crayons?

Tipping the Scales

Elephants march around as if they're the world's biggest animal. Unfortunately for them, that's true only on land: The blue whale is the largest animal anywhere, and by a lot. While the average African elephant weighs around 8,000 pounds, a blue whale weighs about 160 *tons*. A ton is 2,000 pounds, so that's over 300,000 pounds—a lot bigger than an elephant. Not that the difference matters much: If you had both animals as pets, you wouldn't want either one to sit on you.

Wee ones: If an elephant weighs 8,000 pounds, and your car weighs 3,000 pounds, how much more does the elephant weigh?

Little kids: A ton is 2,000 pounds. If an elephant weighs 8,000 pounds, how many tons is that?

Big kids: If you have a pet whale that weighs 160 tons, how many 4-ton elephants would you need to match the weight of the whale?

Answers: 5,000 pounds more; 4 tons; 40 elephants.

23

No Cheetah-ing

Cheetahs aren't the biggest land animal, but they're definitely the fastest. For short distances they can sprint up to 75 miles an hour. That means they're zooming faster than the cars on a highway, and without ever getting a speeding ticket. Cheetahs have to be quick because the animals they eat, like gazelles and zebras, are really speedy themselves—and if you have to run to catch your meal, you'd better be able to keep up.

Wee ones: Cheetahs typically eat only once every 3 days. If you feed your pet cheetah on a Sunday, how many *more* times will it have eaten by the next Sunday?

Little kids: If a cheetah runs 60 miles an hour, and you're driving your car at 70 miles an hour, by how many miles an hour are you barely staying ahead?

Big kids: Suppose your pet cheetah runs 75 miles an hour all the time. If you could ride your pet cheetah to school, and you normally drive there at 25 miles an hour, how many times as fast would the cheetah bring you there?

Another Kind of Water Shooter

Penguins have a lot of charm, and not just because of their cute black-and-white outfits. It's also the way they waddle, thanks to legs that are almost too short to do the job. Fortunately, they are excellent swimmers and great slide-down-the-ice-on-your-belly-ers. Those of us who have an easier time walking than swimming can only dream of zooming through the water like a penguin. We might be able to keep up on the belly sliding, though.

Wee ones: If a penguin shuffles forward 4 feet, takes a rest from all that work, and then shuffles another 5 feet, how many feet forward did it move?

Little kids: If you race against your pet penguin, and you both run/waddle 5 feet to the edge of a cliff, belly-slide 13 feet down the slope, then splash into the water and shoot 20 more feet, over how many feet did you race?

Big kids: If your penguin walks 10 feet in a minute, but slides twice as fast as it walks and swims 4 times as fast as it slides, how many feet per minute does it swim?

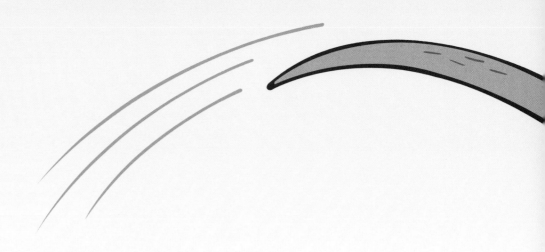

Getting a Jump on It

Thanks to their big, strong hind legs, kangaroos can leap up to 30 feet with a running start. The biggest kind, the red kangaroo, can spring as far as 40 feet! And kangaroos don't just jump far, they fly high—almost 9 feet up into the air. If you could jump that far and that high, you could get around the house a lot faster than you do walking, but you'd hit your head on the ceiling more, too.

Wee ones: A kangaroo has 4 legs. How many legs do a mama kangaroo and the baby in her pouch have together?

Little kids: If a kangaroo takes 3 giant leaps and each leap is 20 feet long, how far does the kangaroo travel?

Big kids: If cars are 6 feet wide, how many cars parked side by side could your pet kangaroo clear with a 24-foot leap?

Spiking Your Dinner

Sometimes food is hard to eat with your hands, especially if it's wet, slippery, or worse yet, alive. But that's exactly what a praying mantis faces at every meal. This insect catches and eats other insects, using front legs that are covered with scratchy spikes. When mantises jump on a tasty insect that has come too close, those prickles help catch and hold the bug while they chow down. It's just as well you don't have spikes on *your* arms, since it would make it hard to pull on a shirt— fortunately, you don't need them to hold down your hamburger.

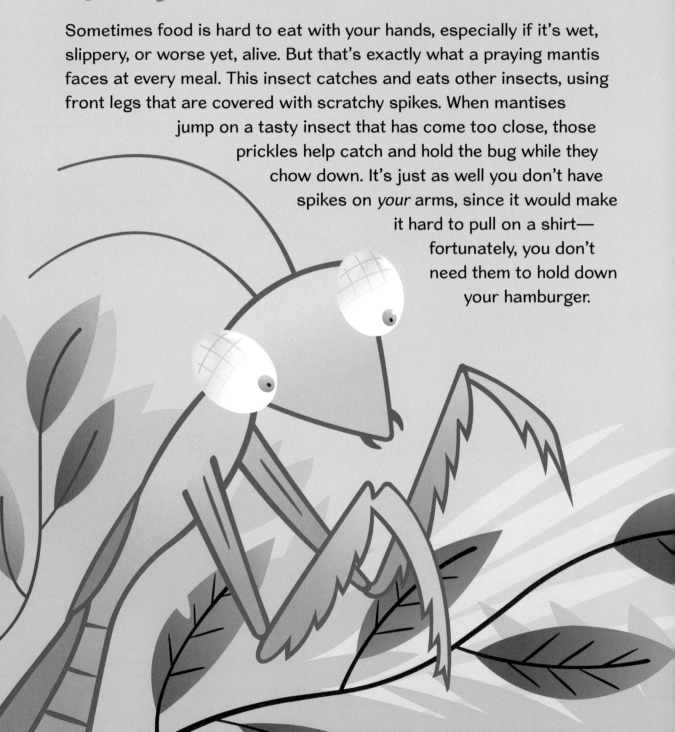

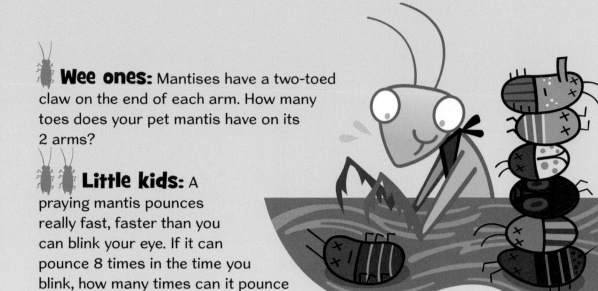

Wee ones: Mantises have a two-toed claw on the end of each arm. How many toes does your pet mantis have on its 2 arms?

Little kids: A praying mantis pounces really fast, faster than you can blink your eye. If it can pounce 8 times in the time you blink, how many times can it pounce when you blink twice?

Big kids: If your pet mantis catches the target bug on its 1st pounce and every 4th time after that, will it catch one on its 19th pounce?

Answers: 4 toes; 16 pounces; No—it will catch one on its 17th and 21st pounce.

31

Stand-Up Routine

The flamingo is one of the most intriguing birds, especially for its wild pink color and its ability to stand on one foot for hours. Flamingos are pink because they eat shrimp, but scientists aren't sure why the birds stand on one leg. One theory is that the flamingo lets half of its body rest, then switches legs so the other half can rest. That doesn't sound like the way we humans take naps—after all, we have trouble balancing on one leg even when we're awake.

Wee ones: If you eat 3 shrimp for dinner and your pet flamingo eats 10, how many shrimp do the two of you eat altogether?

Little kids: You and your pet flamingo compete to see who can stand on one leg longer. If you last 5 seconds without falling over and the flamingo lasts 17 seconds, how much longer did the flamingo last?

Big kids: If you have a whole flock of 20 flamingos, and half are standing on 1 foot while half are standing on 2 feet, how many flamingo feet are on the ground?

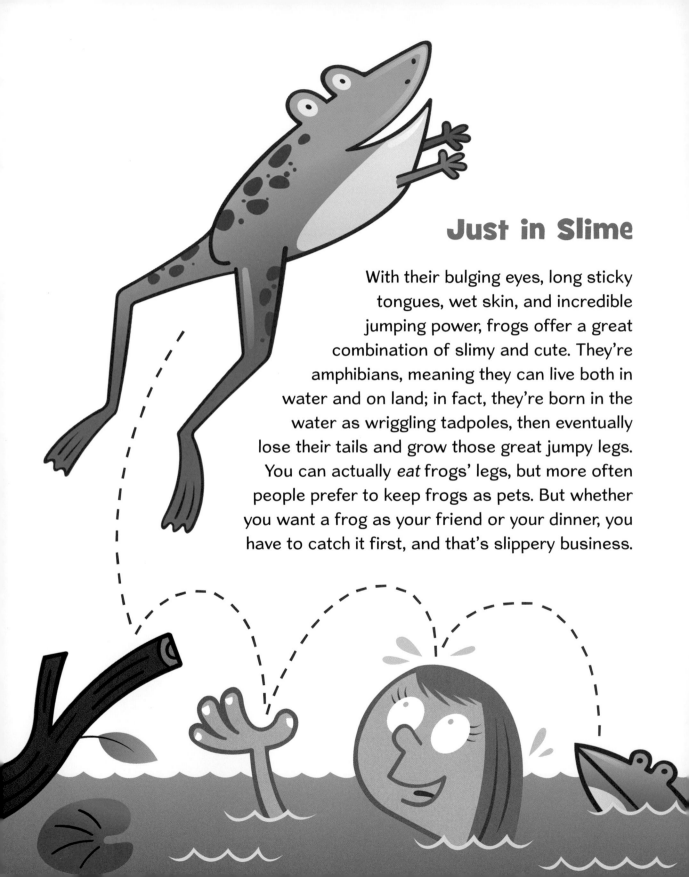

Just in Slime

With their bulging eyes, long sticky tongues, wet skin, and incredible jumping power, frogs offer a great combination of slimy and cute. They're amphibians, meaning they can live both in water and on land; in fact, they're born in the water as wriggling tadpoles, then eventually lose their tails and grow those great jumpy legs. You can actually *eat* frogs' legs, but more often people prefer to keep frogs as pets. But whether you want a frog as your friend or your dinner, you have to catch it first, and that's slippery business.

Wee ones: You're stuck chasing your 3 pet frogs. If the first does 3 jumps, the second does 4 jumps, and the third does 1 jump, how many jumps do they all do before you catch them?

Little kids: Frogs also swim well. If you chase your pet frog and it jumps for 7 feet, then dives into the pool and swims for 12 feet, how many feet did it travel?

Big kids: The Australian rocket frog can jump about 50 times its body length. If the frog is 2 inches long, how many inches can it jump?

Chapter 3

EXTREME VEHICLES

2 26 9 56 116 10 4 18 35 8 63 1

Hosed Down

Fire trucks have a lot of cool equipment, but one of the best parts may be the hose. When firefighters connect it to a fire hydrant, water gushes through the hose to the truck, then back out to another set of hoses that put out the fire. Those hoses have to shoot streams of water that go extremely high and hit the fire all at once, so they blast *really* hard. If you used a fire hose to wash the family car, you'd certainly get the job done faster—but the car could end up on the other side of town.

Wee ones: If a fire truck has 1 hose going into the truck and 4 hoses coming back out, how many hoses does it have?

Little kids: If you can spray your brother with a garden hose from 5 feet away, and a fire hose shoots 10 times as far, from how far away could you spray him with the fire hose?

Big kids: If you hose down a whole parking lot of cars starting at 2:30 pm and it takes you an hour and a half, when do you finish?

Really Mixed Up

If you've ever driven past a construction site, you've probably seen a cement mixer. It's that giant truck with the big, round, rotating bin that drips goopy cement out the back end. A cement mixer can hold over a thousand gallons of mixture—and if you swapped out all that goop for something more appealing, like brownie batter or cookie dough, you could make quite a load of dessert. Maybe these machines belong in the kitchen.

Wee ones: If you have 8 mixer trucks, and 4 are churning cement while the rest are mixing brownie batter, how many are mixing brownies? (Be sure you eat from the right one.)

Little kids: If you start baking all the cookies from a cement mixer at 11:00 am and it takes you 3 hours, when do you finish?

Big kids: Suppose your cement mixer can mix 2,000 gallons of cookie dough. If 1 gallon of cookie dough can make 8 trays of chocolate chip cookies, how many trays of cookies can you pump out of that mixer?

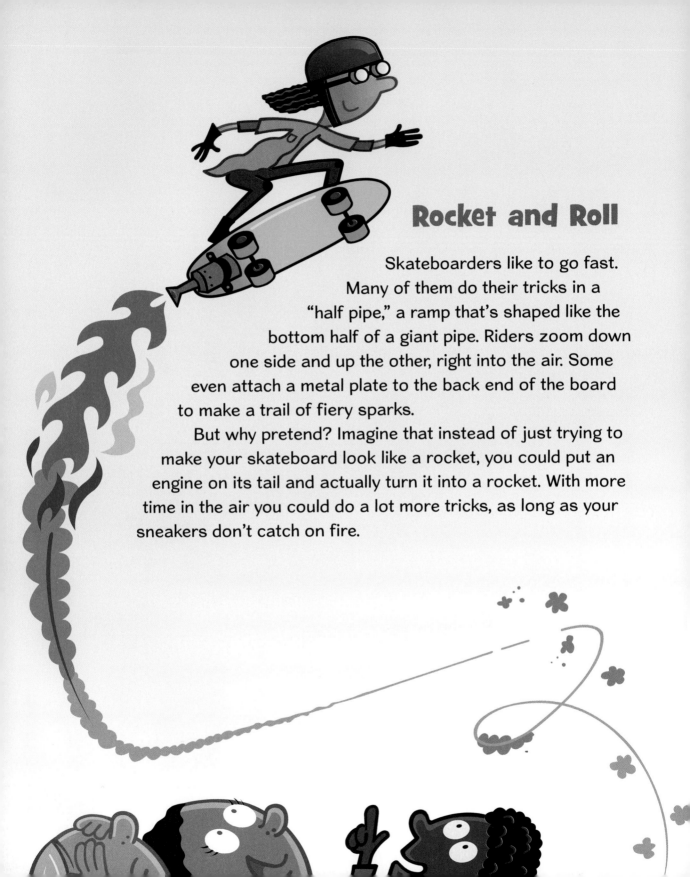

Rocket and Roll

Skateboarders like to go fast. Many of them do their tricks in a "half pipe," a ramp that's shaped like the bottom half of a giant pipe. Riders zoom down one side and up the other, right into the air. Some even attach a metal plate to the back end of the board to make a trail of fiery sparks.

But why pretend? Imagine that instead of just trying to make your skateboard look like a rocket, you could put an engine on its tail and actually turn it into a rocket. With more time in the air you could do a lot more tricks, as long as your sneakers don't catch on fire.

Wee ones: If a rocket skateboarder does 2 spins, plants 2 handstands, and eats a donut while in the air, how many tricks does he do?

Little kids: If a boy rides the rocket skateboard and goes sailing over 5 trees, but a girl tries it and—because she weighs less—she makes it over 13 trees, how many more trees did the girl skateboarder sail over?

Big kids: If it takes you 20 minutes to skateboard to school, but the rocket skateboard zooms 10 times as fast, how many minutes does it take you on the rocket skateboard?

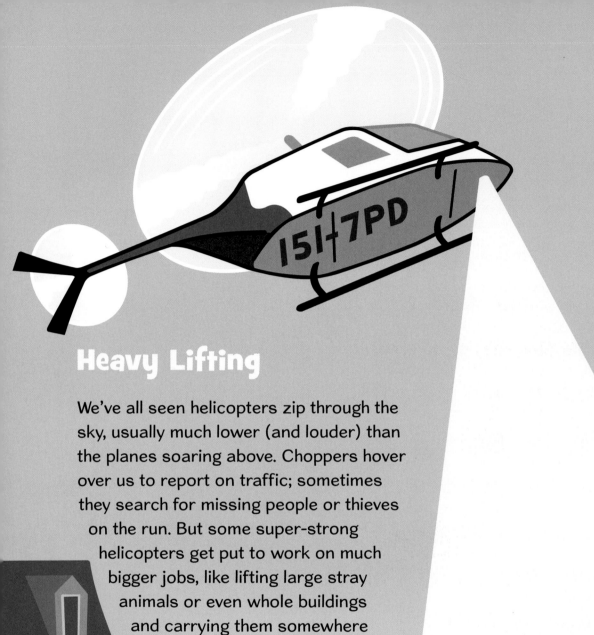

Heavy Lifting

We've all seen helicopters zip through the sky, usually much lower (and louder) than the planes soaring above. Choppers hover over us to report on traffic; sometimes they search for missing people or thieves on the run. But some super-strong helicopters get put to work on much bigger jobs, like lifting large stray animals or even whole buildings and carrying them somewhere else. If one of those flies low overhead, you'd better get out of the way.

Wee ones: If a helicopter airlifts 4 lost rhinos and 3 stranded hippos to safety in one day, how many big endangered animals does it save?

Little kids: If a rhino weighs 5,000 pounds and a hippo weighs 8,000 pounds, how many pounds of animal does the helicopter lift if it picks up one of each?

Big kids: If a super-chopper can lift 2 trucks, and each truck weighs the same as 20 baby hippos, how many baby hippos could that helicopter lift at once?

Scream Machine

Usually if something frightens us, we avoid it. But for some reason, we happily ride roller coasters to scare ourselves on purpose. When you're staring straight down from the top of the rails, and you know you're about to shoot toward earth at full speed and maybe flip upside down after that, there's not much you can do except holler. Since coasters can fall from as high as 400 feet and race as fast as 150 miles per hour, an obvious thing to do in that situation is to scream.

Wee ones: If a roller coaster has 5 big drops and 1 loop-de-loop, how many chances to scream will you get?

Little kids: If your roller coaster car holds 12 people, and half of them are screaming after the first drop, how many people are screaming?

Big kids: If the fastest roller coaster goes 150 miles an hour, and the fastest you've been driven in a car on the road is 80 miles an hour, how much faster does the coaster go?

Under Pressure

A bucket of water can feel pretty heavy. And water feels much, much heavier thousands of feet under the ocean: The pressure is so strong that if you swam down that deep, it would crush you like a pile of cars on top of you. But people want to travel to the ocean floor, mainly to study the wild sea creatures that live there. So scientists need to go down in special super-strong submarines that won't collapse into a pile of junk. If you're willing to work in a cramped steel ball and sink 3 miles deep into pitch-black water, this could be the job for you.

Wee ones: If your deep-sea vehicle heads 3 miles straight down and then rises back up to the surface, how many miles have you traveled?

Little kids: If you build a dozen deep-sea vehicles and toss them into the ocean to see how they'll do, and 5 of them get totally crushed, how many come back up good as new? (Reminder: A dozen equals 12.)

Big kids: Here on land, the air presses your skin with about 14 pounds of force on each square inch. Two miles underwater, the pressure is almost 3 *tons*. Given that a ton is 2,000 pounds, how many pounds press down on one square inch of you when 2 miles below?

Winging It

Flying in a plane—basically hurtling through the sky inside a metal tube—sounds pretty crazy when you stop to think about it. How much crazier is it to strap a jet engine onto your back and fly like *that*? One ex-pilot, Yves Rossy, has done it many times: He's jumped out of planes 7,500 feet above the ground, and flown for 9 minutes at almost 200 miles an hour wearing a jet pack. If you wanted to borrow his jet pack, you'd need a special suit so the jet exhaust doesn't burn you up, and a parachute to land safely from thousands of feet above the ground. Other than that, you'd be totally safe.

Wee ones: If you rocket into the air with your jet pack and fly straight for 2 minutes, then do 6 minutes of loop-de-loops, for how long do you fly?

Little kids: If you jump out of a plane at 7,000 feet and blast upward another 2,000 feet, how many feet high did you fly? (Hint: Think of it in chunks of thousands.)

Big kids: If you're flying at 180 miles an hour, then slow down to 120 miles an hour to open your parachute, by how many miles an hour did you slow down?

2 **83** **7** **34** 22 6 **42** **116** **35** | **14** 92

Chapter 4

SPORTS YOU SHOULDN'T TRY AT HOME

5 26 78 51 106 9 27 ◎ 82 37 45

The Buck Stops Here

Most people don't like to be told what to do, and animals like it even less. The one who likes it the least could be the bull, a male cow with big horns and an even bigger attitude. If you're looking for an animal that doesn't want anyone riding him, a bull is a good choice. In a bull-riding contest, you have to hang on with just one hand and stay on the furious, bucking bull for 8 seconds in order to score points. The bull gets points, too, for kicking his hardest to buck you off.

Wee ones: If you're riding a bull and you've hung on for 5 seconds so far, how many more seconds do you have to ride him to reach 8 seconds and score points?

Little kids: Each judge scores you *and* your bull, with up to 25 points for each of you. If you score 20 points, but your bull scores only 15 for making it too easy, how many more points did you score than the bull?

Big kids: If there are 4 judges and each one can give you up to 25 points, what's the biggest score you can get?

High as a Kite

If you're the kind of person who's always wanted to fly off a mountain, then do we have the sport for you: hang gliding. You strap yourself into a large, winged, kite-shaped object that weighs almost nothing. Then you get a running start and run right off the cliff. If the wind catches you just right, you can soar like a bird for miles. Of course, while the hang glider moves slowly enough to land safely, landing *where* you want to is another story.

Wee ones: If you jump off the cliff and glide 2 miles straight ahead, then turn left and glide another 4 miles, how many miles did you glide through the air?

Little kids: If your house is 20 miles from the cliff, but you stay up in the air only 16 miles before landing, how many miles do you have to walk to get home?

Big kids: If you start flying at 3:20 in the afternoon and stay up in the air for 50 minutes, when do you land?

Stick Figures

There are all kinds of ways we use poles: to push boats, to raise flags, to prop up tree houses. But one of the most fun things to do with a pole is to fling yourself into the air. In the pole vault, you hold a 15-foot-long pole and run full speed at a bar held high up in the air. Then you stick the front tip of the pole into the ground and hang on for your life as the pole flings you upward—until you let go. Then you hope you sail over the bar without knocking into it. The record high is 20 feet 1 inch off the ground, almost as tall as a two-story building . . . so if you're looking to jump over your house, this could do the trick.

Wee ones: If you run with a 7-foot pole and fly over a bar that's 2 feet higher than that, how high a bar did you clear?

Little kids: If you start with the bar 14 feet high for your 1st try, then raise it 1 foot at a time with each jump, how high is the bar for your 4th try?

Big kids: If you try to clear the bar 26 times and knock the bar off only half the time, how many times did you make it over?

Crash Course

Some of the most exciting sports are the ones that take something that's already dangerous—like driving a snowmobile—and then have 20 people race them all crowded together so it's even more dangerous. Snowmobiles can drive at over 100 miles per hour, and they're really hard to control on slippery snow, especially with 19 other snowmobiles zooming around you. If that isn't enough danger, there's freestyling, where contestants drive the snowmobiles off ramps and flip upside down—and hopefully land right side up.

Wee ones: If you flip your snowmobile backward off 2 ramps, then jump it off 3 more ramps while standing up and using no hands, how many ramps did you jump in total?

Little kids: If you jump off 6 ramps on your snowmobile and spend 3 seconds in the air each time, how many seconds do you spend in the air?

Big kids: If 20 snowmobilers race down the hill and there are 3 crashes, with each crash knocking out 2 snowmobiles, how many snowmobiles make it to the bottom?

Diving Right In

There are many ways to jump into a pool, like curling into a ball to make a giant splash, or doing a belly flop smack onto the water. Those can hurt, though, if you hit the water the wrong way. So imagine how carefully you have to jump into a pool from more than 30 feet high! In Olympic diving, divers leap off a superhigh diving board, and as they fall they do all kinds of fancy tricks in the air: twists, spins, and somersaults. Then the trick is to point your body in the right direction before hitting the water—after all that turning, it's hard to know which way is up.

Wee ones: If you want to do 4 somersaults on your way down, and you've done 1 somersault and a twist, how many more somersaults do you still need to do?

Little kids: If you dive head down, and then do 2½ somersaults, will you splash into the water headfirst or feetfirst?

Big kids: If you can squeeze 4 somersaults into a 30-foot dive, how many can you fit into a 60-foot dive if you turn at the same rate?

Stretching the Truth

Even if you aren't afraid of heights, walking on a really high bridge can give you a scare. If that isn't enough of a thrill, you can take a long, elastic cord called a bungee, hook one end to the bridge, hook the other end to yourself, and jump. You then fall at a frightening speed until the bungee stretches enough to pull on you, at which point you get yanked back up—at full speed—toward the sky. Then you slow down, stop in midair, and fall again. Let's just say, if you're going to measure your own bungee cord for this, you'd better do the math right.

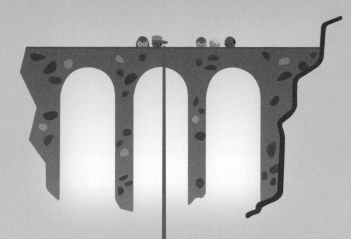

Wee ones: If you fall for 5 seconds before the bungee stops you, then you shoot upward for 4 seconds, how many seconds have you gone flying so far?

Little kids: If the bungee cord is 13 feet long and can stretch to twice that length while holding your weight, how long will it be at full stretch?

Big kids: If you're bungee jumping off a 100-foot-high bridge, and your bungee starts at 37 feet long, how many more feet can it stretch without letting you smack into the ground?

Bus Stop

Your friendly everyday yellow school bus has to be pretty big to hold all those kids. A bus is about 36 feet long and weighs around 28,000 pounds—about ten times more than a car! That's why the World's Strongest Man competition has people *pull* a bus to show that they're strong. The contestant straps himself to the front of the bus, then leans forward and just starts walking to pull the bus 100 feet. Sounds pretty simple, except it takes a *lot* of leg strength to roll 28,000 pounds of bus. Let's hope someone remembered to turn off the brakes.

🚌 **Wee ones:** If your school bus runs out of gas and the driver asks you and 4 friends to pull it, how many of you in total are pulling the bus?

🚌🚌 **Little kids:** If you start pulling your bus and after 40 feet you just have to take a rest, how many more feet do you have to go to pull it to 100 feet?

🚌🚌🚌 **Big kids:** You decide the bus is too easy, so you try pulling a small airplane with your teeth—which some people have done. If the plane weighs twice as much as a 28,000-pound bus, how much does the plane weigh?

Say Cheese!

In England, many towns hold a strange event called Cheese Rolling. People crowd together at the top of a wide, grassy hill, while someone throws a big round wheel of cheese down the slope. Once the cheese rolls a few feet, the race begins, and with a roar everyone starts chasing the cheese. The cheese bounces and rolls *really* fast, so the people have to fling themselves on the ground and roll like logs to keep up. Lots of bruises, lots of broken bones, but the first person who reaches the cheese gets to keep it—which is way more exciting than just buying one at the store.

Wee ones: If the cheese has to roll 10 seconds before people can chase it, and it has rolled for 6 seconds, how long before you can start chasing the cheese?

Little kids: If the cheese rolls for 20 seconds before it crashes into a tree and stops, and the winner reaches it 20 seconds after that, how long after the cheese started rolling did he catch it?

Big kids: If 50 people start chasing the cheese, but 13 get so bruised and banged up that they never reach the bottom of the hill, how many people make it to the end?

47 5 83 4 29 32 2 15 108 9 21 10

Chapter 5

REALLY ODD JOBS

30 2 38 71 26 5 93 44 3 52 36

Pool School

If you want to tell animals what to do, it will go over better if they get a snack for it every time. Exotic animal trainers train the creatures who perform tricks at the zoo, a job that takes a ton of patience. The trainers have to ignore any behavior that doesn't follow instructions—which is most of the time—and give lots of snacks and pats on the back for any trick the animal does right. It's hard enough getting your little brother or sister to stay out of your room; now try getting a sea lion or a dolphin to balance a ball on its nose.

Wee ones: If you get the seal to splash the audience 6 times, but then she also splashes you twice, how many splashes did the seal make?

Little kids: If you throw the ball to the sea lion, and he catches it on his nose the 3rd time and every 3rd throw after that, does he catch the ball on the 13th throw?

Big kids: If you and your dolphins start your show at 1:45 pm and it lasts 20 minutes, when do you finish?

Pressure Cooker

If you've ever been to a diner where you could see the cooks cooking, you know what a crazy job that is. Short-order cooks cook food that will be served in a short amount of time—hence the name—and it's usually a mad scramble. They're cooking burgers, hot dogs, eggs, and pancakes all at once, all requiring different timing, and all in a rush. As the cook runs the griddle, the toaster, and the milk shake machine, it's a miracle that any food comes out cooked right at all.

Wee ones: If the griddletop can fit 4 pancakes, 3 eggs, and 2 burgers, how many items are you cooking at the same time?

Little kids: If the steak for steak and eggs takes 10 minutes to cook, and the eggs take only 4 minutes, how many minutes after starting the steak should you start the eggs to finish at the same time?

Big kids: If pancakes take 8 minutes to cook and burgers take 5 minutes, which will take you longer, 3 rounds of pancakes in a row or 5 rounds of burgers?

Getting a LEGO® Up

When you open a new set of LEGO® building bricks, it's fun to follow the instructions and build that car, castle, or jet plane before you lose any pieces. Some sets get really complicated: You have to add lots of tiny pieces in just the right places, or angles won't line up and propellers won't spin. Just think, as hard as it can be to build it, someone else first had to plan the whole thing: What object the set should make, what colors it should be, what funky pieces it should use. That person is called a LEGO® designer. But even with all those decisions, being a LEGO® designer isn't all work and no play.

Wee ones: If you build a LEGO® car that seats 3 minifigures in the front row, 3 in the middle row, and 3 in the back, how many minifigures can ride in the car?

Little kids: If you have to design an Egyptian temple with just 25 pieces, and you already know the roof will need 10 of them, how many pieces are left for the rest of the building?

Big kids: If you're designing a castle that uses 200 pieces, and a quarter of them have to be pink, how many pink pieces do you have to throw in there?

Answers: 9 LEGO® minifigures; 15 pieces; 50 pink pieces.

Weather or Not

The great thing about being a meteorologist, or weather forecaster, is that no one ever notices whether you're doing your job right. The map goes up, the weather guy/gal tells us what temperature it's going to be tomorrow and whether it's going to rain, or shine, and then that's it—we never see what they said *yesterday* and whether that's what actually happened. Any job where no one checks how well you're doing must be the best job in the world, but if someone starts tracking the numbers, these people are going to be in trouble.

SUNNY ALL DAY!

Wee ones: If the weatherman says it will rain every day this week but it rains just 1 day, how many days was the forecast wrong?

Little kids: If the temperature was supposed to be 74 degrees and it's 51 degrees instead, how far off was the weatherwoman?

Big kids: If the weatherman predicts that it will rain ½ the days in April, but only ⅓ of the days are rainy, how many days were called wrong? (Reminder: April has 30 days.)

Getting Fired

A cannon is a big, heavy metal object with a hollow tube that shoots big objects, usually cannonballs. At the circus and other events, though, sometimes they light the cannon and a *person* comes flying out over everyone's head. It is a real, living person, and this is a real job you could do. Luckily they don't fire the cannon by making something explode inside it; usually there's a giant spring or a jet of air that pushes the person out. But that's little comfort when you're about to sail through the air at over 100 miles an hour.

CAND

Wee ones: If they fire off your cannon 8 times but 4 of those times it fizzles out and doesn't work, how many times do you shoot out of the cannon?

Little kids: If you shoot out of the cannon at 100 miles an hour, and you normally drive in a car at 50 miles an hour, how much faster did you fly than you drive?

Big kids: The world record for a human cannonball is 193 feet. If you build a cannon that shoots you twice as far, how far will you fly?

Game Changer

If you watch a football game closely, you might notice someone running around in a large animal costume, waving its arms to get the crowd to cheer. That crazy person is the team mascot, and the costume usually matches the team name—a lion for the Lions, a bear for the Bears, and so on. It isn't all fun and games being the mascot, though. The suit is really thick and furry so kids can pat him, and the holes for the eyes barely line up to let the person see. Really, the job might be hotter and sweatier than actually playing football on the field.

Wee ones: If you're the team's mascot—a lion—and you do 5 cartwheels for the crowd but the head falls off your costume twice, for how many cartwheels does your head stay on?

Little kids: If you lead the crowd in the team song 7 times and then do 5 dance numbers with the cheerleaders, how many musical numbers did you perform?

Big kids: If your team plays 28 games in a season, and at half the games the other team's mascot tackles you to rile up the crowd, at how many games do you get tackled?

For the Dogs

Walking a dog can be challenging, especially when it's a puppy who hasn't "been trained" yet and who keeps stopping to sniff things on the street, like hydrants, bags of garbage, and other dogs' rear ends. But try walking ten dogs! In cities where lots of people live on one street block, it's easy for a professional dog walker to pick up a whole herd of pooches from people's houses and apartments, and walk them all at once. As we'll see, that requires some planning.

Wee ones: If the dog walker picks up 2 poodles at the first home, 3 beagles at the second home, and a large mutt at the third, how many dogs is he/she walking in total?

Little kids: If a dog walker has 10 dogs, but has leashes to walk only 4 dogs at a time, how many trips does it take to walk all the dogs?

Big kids: The dog walker has to walk 40 dogs today, which is pretty much impossible to begin with. To top it off, ½ the dogs want to fetch balls, another ⅕ of them want to play Frisbee, and 3 others want to eat dog treats. How many dogs actually want to walk like they're supposed to?

Sniff
Sniff

Title	Wee ones	Little kids	Big kids
Hot, Hot, Hot	8-3=5	3,500-2,500=1,000	35,000/3,500=10
Playing Ketchup	3+1=4	1+3+3+3=10	14x2=28
Pop Culture	10-3=7	15-9=6	2x13=26
Eggstreme Mess	2+2=4	10x3=30	30-17=13
Totally Squashed	4+5=9	1,000x5=5,000	4x900=3,600, 5x700=3,500
Shaken Bottle	10-5=5	40/10=4	(60-42)/2=9
See What Sticks	9-2=7	18-10=8	8+(8/4)=10
The 10-Second Rule	8-6=2	12-8=4	120/2=60
Local Color	2+2+1=5	20x2=40	24-9=15
Tipping the Scales	8,000-3,000=5,000	8,000/2,000=4	160/4=40
No Cheetah-ing	6/3=2	70-60=10	75/25=3
Another Kind of Water Shooter	4+5=9	5+13+20=38	10x2x4=80
Getting a Jump on It	4+4=8	3x20=60	24/6=4
Spiking Your Dinner	2+2=4	8x2=16	1+4+4+4+4=17+4=21
Stand-Up Routine	3+10=13	17-5=12	(20/2)x1+(20/2)x2=30
Just in Slime	3+4+1=8	7+12=19	50x2=100
Hosed Down	1+4=5	5x10=50	2:30+1½ hrs=4:00
Really Mixed Up	8-4=4	11:00+3 hrs=2:00	2,000x8=16,000
Rocket and Roll	2+2+1=5	13-5=8	20/10=2
Heavy Lifting	4+3=7	5,000+8,000=13,000	2x20=40
Scream Machine	5+1=6	12/2=6	150-80=70
Under Pressure	3+3=6	12-5=7	2,000x3=6,000
Winging It	2+6=8	7,000+2,000=9,000	180-120=60
The Buck Stops Here	8-5=3	20-15=5	25x4=100
High as a Kite	2+4=6	20-16=4	3:20+50 min=4:10
Stick Figures	7+2=9	14+3=17	26/2=13
Crash Course	2+3=5	6x3=18	20-(3x2)=14
Diving Right In	4-1=3	2½ turns	4x2=8
Stretching the Truth	5+4=9	13x2=26	100-37=63
Bus Stop	4+1=5	100-40=60	28,000x2=56,000
Say Cheese!	10-6=4	20+20=40	50-13=37
Pool School	6+2=8	no, 13 not a multiple of 3	1:45+20 min=2:05
Pressure Cooker	4+3+2=9	10-4=6	8x3<5x5
Getting a LEGO® Up	3+3+3=9	25-10=15	200/4=50
Weather or Not	7-1=6	74-51=23	(30/2)-30/3=5
Getting Fired	8/2=4	100-50=50	193x2=386
Game Changer	5-2=3	7+5=12	28/2=14
For the Dogs	2+3+1=6	4x2<10, so 3	40-(40/2)-(40/5)-3=9